Painting

Are you beginning to find out what you can do with paints, crayons, and papers? This second painting book in the Whitman Creative Art Series is for you. Here are projects to encourage children who have been using art materials and are eager for new and imaginative things to do.

If you are a parent or teacher, the pictures and simple description of each art suggestion given here should help in presenting interesting and creative art experiences. If you are a school-age child, you will enjoy experimenting with these activities and want to use them to express your own ideas and feelings. Many kinds of pictures can grow out of each new way of working!

The children participating in these activities are students in the Wilmette Public Schools, Wilmette, Illinois.

Photographs by Egons Tomsons

WHITMAN HOBBY
DIVISION
Western Publishing Company, Inc.
Racine, Wisconsin
Copyright © 1966 by Western Publishing Company, Inc.
Produced in the U.S.A.

art materials

It is often helpful to organize supplies and clean-up materials in a large box. You will want rags, a sponge, and paint and water containers such as discarded coffee cans, glass jars, and plastic food containers. All kinds of papers can be used for art activities; some large inexpensive papers are newspapers, newsprint, wrapping paper, manila, and colored construction paper. Scissors, paste, and other useful household materials are mentioned on the activity pages. Don't forget pencils, crayons, and chalk!

paint

Tempera and powdered "poster" paints that mix with water are inexpensive and satisfying to work with. Your first colors should be RED, YELLOW, BLUE, BLACK, and WHITE. Other basic colors, GREEN, ORANGE, VIOLET, and BROWN, can be added later.

Pre-mixed tempera paint is sold in jars, ready to use. You must add water to powdered paint before using. Place powder in a container and mix with a little water to make a thick paste. Add more water and a small amount of liquid laundry starch until mixture is thin enough to paint with.

You may wish to include watercolors and finger paints with your paint supplies.

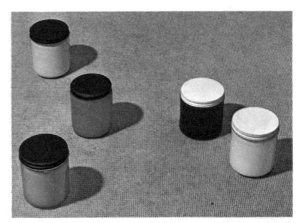

when you are

painting

Your work area can be the kitchen table or any surface that can be cleaned easily. Linoleum floors, and lots of newspaper, are fine for BIG projects!

The best painting tools are sturdy, long-handled art brushes. Paint brushes sold in hardware and paint stores can also be used if the bristles are cut to a one-inch length.

Start with a big brush painting exercise! Use clean water and a large brush to make water designs on a blackboard, a concrete wall, floor, or sidewalk.

When you use your paints, remember to wash brushes in *cold* water and soap after each painting session. Store clean brushes, bristles up, in a can, or wrap them in newspapers. Wet paintings can be hung on a string, wire, or clothesline. Heavily painted pictures should be allowed to dry on a flat surface.

Using a warm iron, press out dry, curled paintings between two sheets of heavy plain paper.

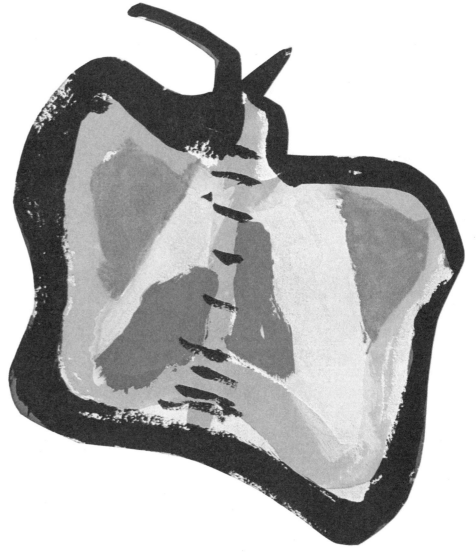

String painting over leaves.

painting

String painting over newspaper shapes.

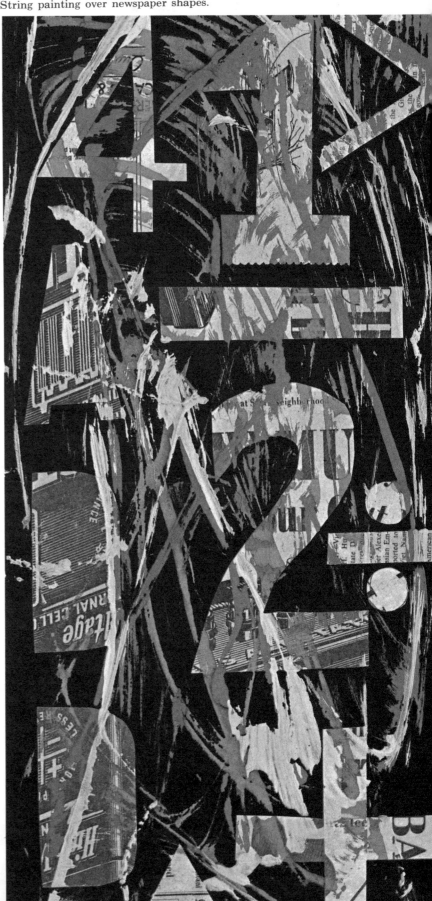

1 Cut or tear shapes from a sheet of paper. Arrange these on any white, black, or colored construction paper. Paste shapes to paper.

2 Drop one end of a cord or string into a container of paint. Pull the string out, squeezing it between a brush and the inside of the can to remove extra paint. Put the wet part of the string on the paper; drag it back and forth to leave a paint pattern over the paper design.

crayons

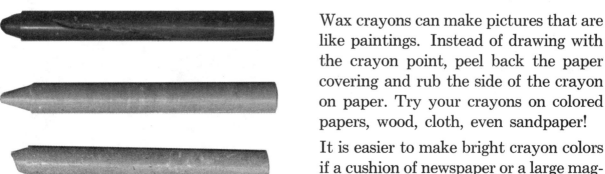

Wax crayons can make pictures that are like paintings. Instead of drawing with the crayon point, peel back the paper covering and rub the side of the crayon on paper. Try your crayons on colored papers, wood, cloth, even sandpaper!

It is easier to make bright crayon colors if a cushion of newspaper or a large magazine is placed under the drawing paper.

Large crayons color big areas.

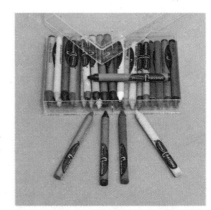

Draw with these pointed crayons.

Did you know that
crayons could be used
in these ways?

side   mix   dark on light colors   outline   hard soft

crayon

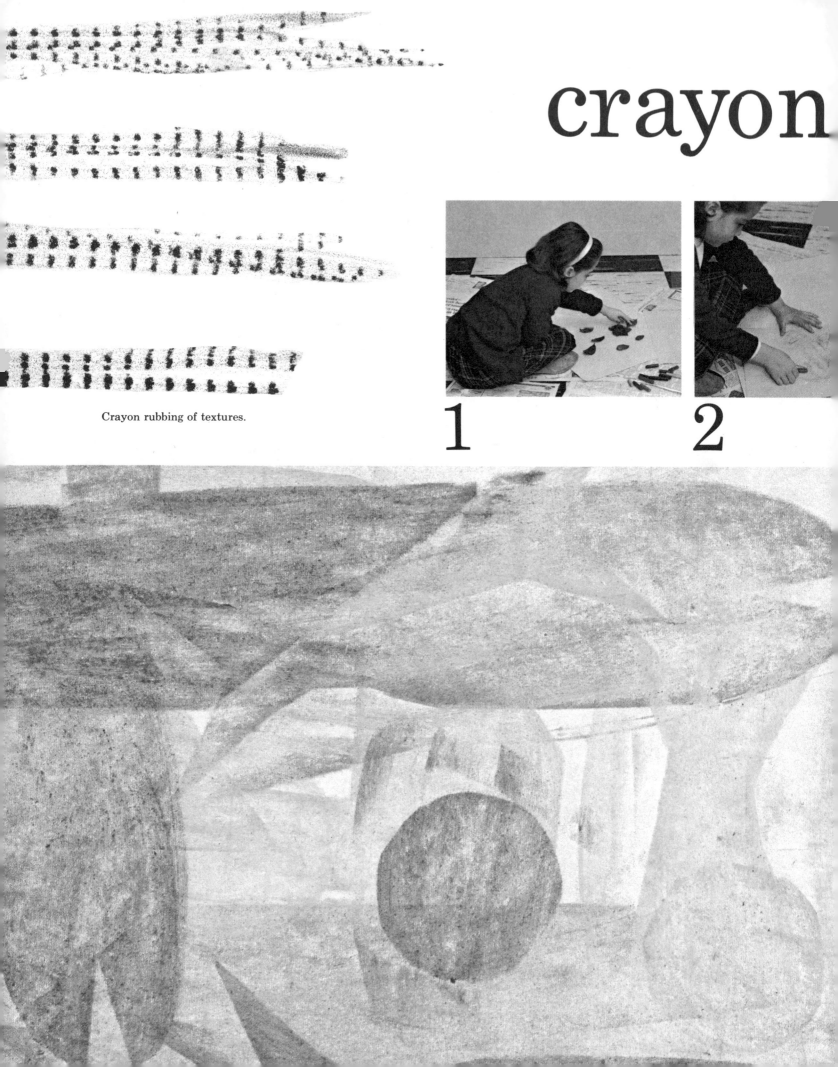

Crayon rubbing of textures.

1

2

rubbing

You need: *newsprint, or any thin paper, and crayons. Also, corrugated paper, sandpaper and other papers, tempera paint, and a brush.*

Look around and touch the things that you see. Wood, stone, leaves — each thing has a different feeling because it has a different surface or texture. "Crayon rubbings" are pictures of each texture.

To make a crayon rubbing of a texture, cover it with a paper and hold this in place with your hand. Rub the side of the crayon across the paper. Find other textures. Try crayon rubbings of bricks, tree bark, metal grills, screens, a penny.

Arrange leaves or cut or torn paper shapes in an interesting design and make a crayon rubbing of this. Move the leaves or papers around, replace the top paper, and rub over this with another crayon color. Thin paint can be brushed over crayon rubbings.

Place wax paper over a white paper and draw on this with a pencil, pressing wax lines into the bottom paper. Brush thin paint over the wax lines and watch a design appear!

Paint brushed over wax lines and shapes.

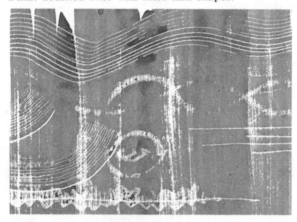

Make a wax crayon picture. Press down on crayons and fill the picture with many colors but leave some areas of white paper. When you brush thin paint over it, your crayon picture should still show. If necessary, add water to the paint.

wax resist

Materials needed: *wax paper, a pencil, white paper, wax crayons, tempera or watercolor paints, a brush.*

Paint over crayon lines; white areas painted with other colors.

crayon

Cover a white paper with one or many crayon colors. Press down to leave a thick layer of color. Completely cover this with black crayon. Now scratch through the black with your tools.

Try another "scratch drawing." This time, rub over the crayon colors with black or violet paint that has a little liquid soap added to it, then "draw" with tools.

1   2

Examples of etching techniques.

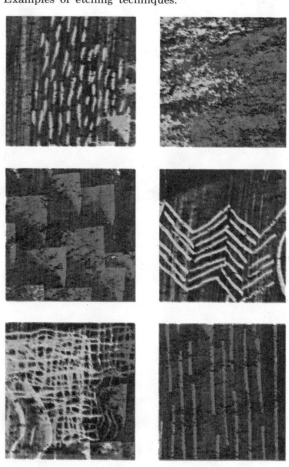

etching

Materials and tools: *wax crayons, paint, white paper, a cloth, and scratching tools.* (Use edge of spoon, scissors, a darning needle, or a nail.) Smooth, heavy paper works best.

3

chalk painting

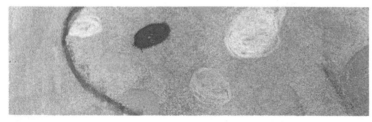

Materials: *soft colored chalks, newsprint, manila, colored construction or white drawing paper, and hair spray.*

Chalk works best for big pictures and designs. Sweep the side of the chalks across the paper. Mix the colors together by blending with tissue or your fingers. If hair spray is used on finished pictures, the chalk will not rub off.

charcoal drawing

You need: *charcoal sticks or dark colored chalks, papers, hair spray.*

Do lots of drawings with this easy material. Press hard to make sharp, dark lines. Make a "soft" picture by rubbing over the lines with a tissue, a rag, or your fingers. Spray the drawings you want to keep.

stencil

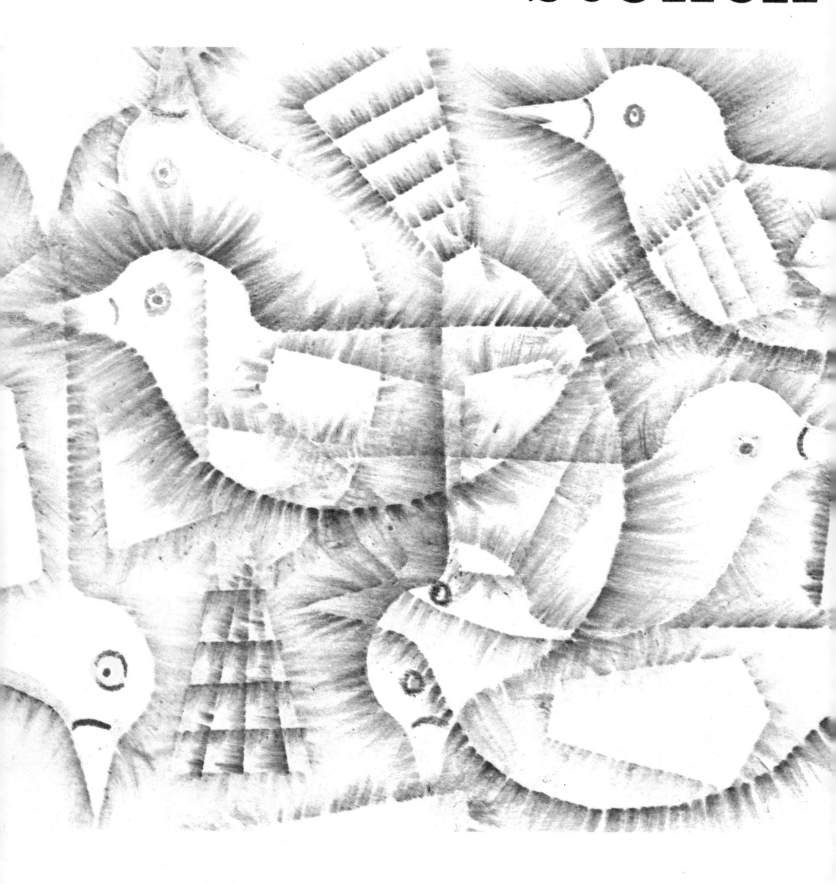

pictures

Materials: *colored chalks, crayons, tissue, scissors, a pencil eraser, and paper. (Hair spray for chalk pictures.)*

Tear or cut out simple paper shapes. A "stencil picture" is an outline of these shapes. Rub a heavy layer of chalk along the edges of the paper stencil. Hold this down on a sheet of paper and with a wad of tissue, brush chalk off the stencil onto the paper. Move the stencil around to make more stencil shapes on your paper.

Make a stencil picture with crayons instead of chalk. Use a pencil eraser to rub crayon onto the paper.

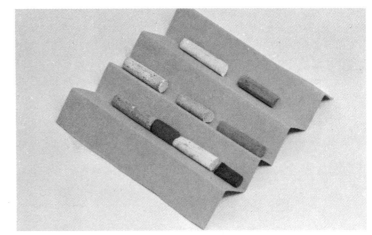

A folded paper holds your crayons and chalks.

1

2

Crush dry paper into a ball. Unfold and spread on a flat surface. Cover the paper with thin tempera or finger paint. Or pour on one tablespoon of liquid laundry starch and sprinkle a little powdered paint on this. Mix and spread the paint, rubbing it into the wrinkles in the paper until a pattern of cracks appears. With a pointed brush, paint over the lines in the paper, then add paint in some of the shapes the lines form.

painting

Materials: *finger-paint paper, finger paints or tempera paints, a pointed brush.* (For finger-paint paper use magazine covers, glazed shelf paper, or any smooth, shiny paper.)

more painting

Make a finger-paint design using finger paints or powdered paint mixed with liquid laundry starch. When this painting is dry, paint over the finger-paint pattern with a pointed brush.

Make your own paint! Mix soap flakes and water into a smooth paste. Add a few drops of food coloring to this and use like finger paint. Combine food coloring with toothpaste or hand lotion to make other homemade paints.

Hand lotion with blue and yellow food coloring.

projects

Cover a paper with a thin film of liquid laundry starch. Sprinkle powdered paint or spoon small pools of liquid paint on several parts of the paper. Cut a piece of cardboard so that it has a notched edge and use this to spread and mix the colors. Make a painting with a comb, a rag, or a piece of sponge. What other things can you use to paint with?

Toothpaste and food coloring.   Soap flakes and food coloring.

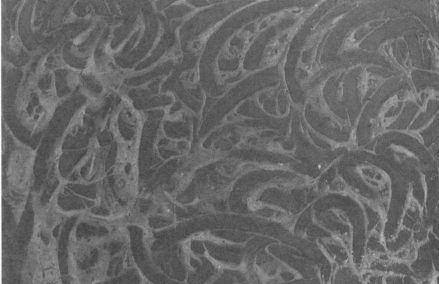

dry brush

1

Cut stencil shapes out of heavy paper or cardboard and arrange on paper. Use both the cut out shapes and the leftover paper frames. Dip brush in paint, then remove most of the paint by wiping the brush on a newspaper before using it. This is called painting with a "dry brush."

stenciling

Materials: *paint, a large brush, scissors, white paper, heavy paper, or cardboard.* Worn-out paint brushes are fine for this project!

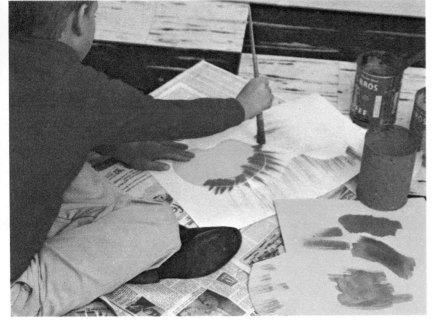

2

Now place the brush on the edge of the stencil and sweep it off the edge onto the paper. Try different colors and other stencil shapes.

melted

crayon

1

2

Here's a way to use up your crayon stubs!

Look for: *crayon pieces, shelf paper, an iron, and a tool to shave or chip crayons.* (A dull knife, a vegetable peeler, or a grater can be used.)Finger-paint paper or any smooth, shiny paper may be used instead of glazed shelf paper.

Chip crayons onto a piece of shelf paper. Place a second piece of paper on top of the sheet with the crayon chips. Use a warm iron to press on this second paper and melt the crayon. After you remove the top paper, you can draw with a black crayon over the melted colors or use your scissors to scratch a line design into the wax.

3

spatter painting

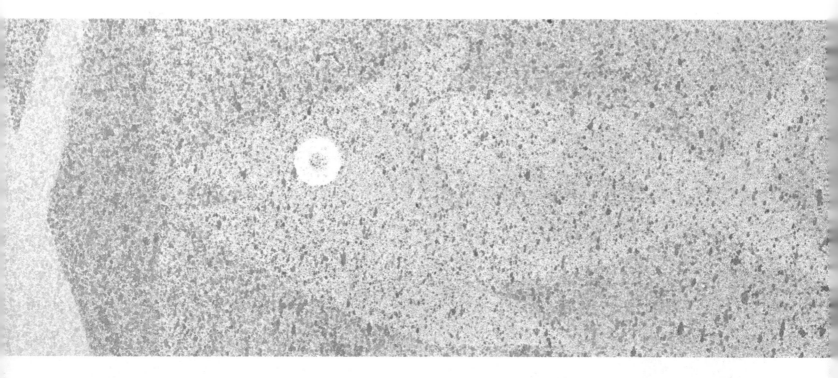

Materials: *insecticide spray gun or other refillable spray bottles such as perfume atomizers or window spray cleaners, papers, scissors, pins, tempera paint, and assorted objects such as leaves, twigs, paper shapes, wire, string, and cloth.*

Fill spray container with thin paint. Cover work area with newspapers and place the paper to be decorated on them. Arrange leaves, grasses, and other things on this paper, pinning down light objects. Hold spray container a short distance from the objects and spatter the paint. Then remove those items and rearrange them or arrange others on the paper and continue to spray with other colors.

A neater way of making small spatter pictures is to pin your paper inside of a box and spray into this.

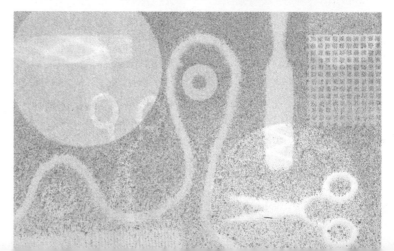